Now
Begin
Again

Now Begin Again

Felipe Mehta

to my Mom.

Now Begin Again

Felipe Mehta

Halbaffe Press

Minneapolis, Minnesota

First published 2024 by
HALBAFFE PRESS

Halbaffe Press in the US is an imprint of Sinensis Publications, a division of Sinensis LLC, registered in the USA.

ISBN-13: 979-8-218-36998-9

midnight at robbie's

Sitting together,
I don't care about
anything
nor anyone else,
I just want
to relive
every second
we sat together,

wish i could have
maintained
eye contact

wish you had said
you were in love with me

it would have
changed everything

reality.

Lying in bed,
next to my mom,
fever of 104
brief, feverish dreams,
in and out
of consciousness,

The only things
that matter
in this life
are other people,

not the degree in advertising
nor the fancy objects,
no matter how they
are inked up.

eternal solitude

trembling with solitude
cannot, will not
acknowledge
my own grief
my own existence

must be strong and resolute
for everyone else

they can rest
I cannot

let go

Found a box
of old stuff

picture frames,
greeting cards,
including,
a handmade card
from you,

you even referred to
the guy i was seeing then

i feel sick now,
didn't realize
in hindsight
how jealous
someone could be

move on!
you have your own life!
there is no competition!

freefall

vivid dreams
nightmares,

filled with fear,
dread,
falling, helplessly
from a pole,
or bungee jumping
a broken elevator,
doesn't matter,

always the same.

electric fear.

You said
you hate
your biological
father,

he sounds
like a monster,

yet you are so
eager
to share
good news
with him
(why mention me?)

but when cornered,
you also
lash out
at women

are you even
different?

burden.

being vaguely aware
of her
ever-present
baggage

these are
her coping skills
for getting through
this time

remember something
get overwhelmed
cry
analyze
repeat.

not a monologue

you want me
to nag you

(i'm not your mother
and i'm not mine, either!)

and maybe
i'm new to this,
but i don't know
why

do i need to
repeat myself?
or just use
a stronger tone?
should i swear?

i'm at a loss...

still flirty.

ma'am, please!

you only want
what's not
on the menu

hot cold
cold hot

you're sane
in every aspect
of your life,
but love

identity theft

I.

Someone
had heard
there was a
religious loophole
for transgender folk:
if they didn't mention it,
we were fine.

Alex, your cousin, argued,
Jesus was obviously gay
(a hushed up
Biblical controversy)
so we had to be accepted too.

I stared in disbelief
"why is your family
so fucked up?"

if only we could
all talk frankly
and obliterate
confusion.

you knew
from experience,
life isn't perfect,
but didn't tell me.

i felt like i lived
under a tiger mom,
you didn't tell me
it was all moms,

living surrounded
by grey cement walls,

yet did your boobs stay?

II.

in spring
I met up with Hera
who had good news.
we sat on a park bench,
as I did her makeup,
after she came out
as transitioning
and wanting to
form a formal community.

I came out as non-binary, too.

We ate pizza
and joked about
gender constructs,

fences,
layers,
between us,
from us,
secretly bitter,
so much had changed
for everyone.

III.

in the full bloom
of that summer,
we screamed
we danced on the cusp
of the joy
amongst the ebb,
the exigencies
of the day

We talked about
the dimensionality
of being gay,
I presented a
four-dimensional model,
like a weather map but
zero regard
for time.

someone introduced us
to their friend, S,
a psycho bitch
we never want
to see again.

Fred bitched that we
had to be strong
then swung out at me.
I was never happy enough
to be called gay

They just wanted me
to admit that i was
at least gay,
if not also trans,
then kick me
out
of the closet.

IV.

One night, I lay in bed,
I felt an Unseen Force,
maybe religion
got it wrong,
maybe He accepted us
after all

now finally,
presented with
the opportunity,
i shirked away,
not sure who I was,

maybe the 4D model
wasn't as accurate
about who I am,
maybe I was
just a really dry
tomboy
or maybe just bi?

being unable
to come out

to my mom,
a homophobe,
was the issue,
stuck with her,
i couldn't bounce ideas,
living an open secret.

I had to feel
like i could come out,
without hormones
without judgement
and still be accepted
as myself.

pacman

I think when
we broke up
you in your
toxic way
put a hex
to keep
others away
from me.

un/fortunately,
the secret
was discovered
and cracked.

if you couldn't
be happy
for me,
forget I exist.

shun me or move on

Never going to leave
though some people
think
I've gone against God
I don't care,
my spiritual
problems
are precisely
between just
me and God.

peace

floating
in a pool
beside you,
i never knew
i could be this happy
though we weren't ideal
for each other,
which is why
it never worked out.

Still love you,
though we
both
moved on

friends

you
wanted me
to talk
the whole
time

so you
could judge
when to pull
away.

thanksss

vacuum of an ex

Knitted anatomical
heart shapes
you are jealous
of everything
you feel
you don't have
but I am also
alone and struggling
Don't bite us
in your search
for happiness.

You are mad
at me now
but maybe
my eyes
will be dry
soon.

still biting

I love you,
and am sorry
but I can't
understand
why you're still
mad at me,
your interpretation
of what happened
wasn't shared with me.

gurl...

You tell me
you have other
commitments,
other friends to see
in front of everyone,
so they think I'm
a heartless wolf who
has hurt you,
as if I really am
in the wrong,
too

goodbye, normalcies

Hanging out with you,
on the eve of,
sitting together
in your living room,
in our beautiful
quiet presence,
before no more.

it's a thing

three in the morning
at the train station,
I'm with Fuck-Frank
(FF for short)
and Bryn shows up,
not sure who he is
or what's up,
then we meet
more strangers,
everyone is
just chill,
looking for snacks,
like old friends
coming together,

in that moment,
you know
you will look
back wistfully
from then on…

little bit

i know it was
out of love
which you equated
with control
but you could
have talked
about it too.

i thought
the whole
point of dating
was to find
ourselves,
but nobody
told you that.

we are not friends anymore

You ditched me
often,
when i needed
you most,
leaving me
more shocked
than hurt.

so maybe you
are more quick
to forgive
for that
reason,

but i am
still a bitch,
don't rub it in

sisterhood

I love you
like a stupid sister,
and I assume
you love me too,

I cannot
tolerate
anything less.

Just because
you are mad
doesn't mean
we don't talk.

Hate me,
blame me,
scream at me
the silence
is deafening.

not good

You are
one of the
smartest people
i know,
but you make
me so mad,
to me you are
unlovable,
such that
you don't
deserve
to be called
a bitch.

cartoon drawing

I can't believe
that we fought
over something
that small
and basic,
as in,
you complain
that your rights
are always
infringed upon,
but you don't
have any
regard for
anyone else.

I love you
too much.
I let you
trample
my heart.

abandoner

i don't mean
to dump
everyone

(rest assured,
you've all been
hurt equally
by me)

but I need
to fix myself
before I
can love
anyone else,

maybe I
don't deserve
friends
until then.

awkward pup

between the times
that I see you
i completely
forget how
bad you are
with expressing
emotions

i have to
share how i
constantly feel
with everyone

with you
i am unheard

you think something
is wrong, broken
if I express myself,

but if i hold it in,
i explode.

do you see me
as an actual
creation
not a slice
of your psyche?

here.

i become
emotional
and you are cold,

do you know

that i need you
to express yourself
too?

if i am
too soft
or too near,
let me know

backbiting

standing in a freezing
parking garage,
fumbling for my keys
around 10pm,
library's closed

every noise
makes me jumpy,

yet you want
to calmly gossip
about our friend,
and their new boyfriend,

i love you dearly,
but can it wait?

heatwave

did you
turn on the oven
or is it
my hormones?

it's the kind
of heat
that can make
a polar bear
like myself
crazy with anger,

i don't know
what the scientists
are saying
anymore

but i can't
last

rhetorically speaking

You lay there
like a fucking
hedonistic chump

I can't tell the difference
between you
and the rabid squirrels
outside.

My barbarian other half,
I can draw you a map
but it's too literal
or not literal enough.
You are intelligent
but don't always
act like it.

You are like a cursed child
I secretly wished for,
but wasn't sure
I actually wanted.

Having equal attention
deficits,
we deserve each other.

brother

I somehow
spent a week
at your house,
your mom
taking care of us,
it just felt so good,
to be in middle school
and have that freedom.

So you came
home with me
for the next week,
and my parents
loved you,
maybe more
than us,
and i actually felt
a little bit jealous.

i didn't say
anything, but you
might have
noticed.

yet it was
glorious
to have a brother,
for once.

looking, forward

Sister, we have
deeper values
in common,
than superficial
interests,

but in the everyday
we don't see that.

I hate that we
neglected to bond

to unfold time
to hold each other
in conversation
again.

sobbing internally.

Texted my mom
came out
as trans,
I thought she understood
what nonbinary meant

She didn't respond.

Didn't see it until
I asked her in person

She accused me
of being confused,
trying to break
a glass ceiling
that doesn't exist.

I sobbed and realized
that cultures
don't transfer
like currency.

No need to

come out
to everyone.
Also, cultures
and ideas,
like languages,
evolve over time.

kiss.

woke up
in the morning
the train empty,
party animals, drunks,
and commuters were gone

saw you in the station,
carrying photos,

biochemical balance,
receptors synced in embrace,
as our eyes met,
and we kissed

when we talked,
it was total confusion,
a bit of gibberish from
everywhere,
don't know where
you came from
stay here.

not today, not ever.

In the throes
of adolescence,
maybe you
didn't know
that i saw you
as only a sister
and bff,
and you thought
we could be
something more?

Something different?

I never
wanted
to hurt you,
that camping trip
was rough on
everyone,

and i don't remember
much after that.

but the pain
i caused you
still hurts me
today.

depth.

as teens,
you and i had to face
reality vs ideals

we wanted to be
perfect adults
but we had
self esteem issues,
internal demons
material burdens
terrible acne,

Likewise,
I know who
my true friends were,
and I would have
fought harder
to keep them,
in retrospect.

what did i do?

we were
in the same
group of friends.

we wrote letters
to each other
later.

but back in 5th grade,
somehow it became
public knowledge
that you wrote in
your diary
about me
having my period

everyone said
it was cool
that you
kept a diary

I was "irrationally"
furious that I
was mentioned

thankfully,
we stuck together.

toxic.

when we went
anywhere,
i was always
the unofficial
boyfriend
some kind of
female tomboy
arm-candy

even with other
female friends,
they treated me
like a boyfriend,
following along,
passively
disinterested.

you couldn't bring
yourself to come out
or have any kind
of relationship with
anyone else
as fucked as ours.

afterlife

to feel again,
the vibrating
blue
(like _____)

the fortifying
breeze
through
our hair

my two lips
against
your downy
cheek

relationship poem

Luminous orbs
we float
we graze
past each other
acknowledgement
barely registering
for even
a second.

So anyways,

Then one day
I was sitting
in a coffee shop
warming up
and suddenly
an idea hit me

I have a cousin
in Singapore
I had stayed
with her before
in 2015

I made a call
she said sure!

Printed in the USA
CPSIA information can be obtained
at www.ICGtesting.com
CBHW052326130924
14210CB00014B/208

9 798218 369989